The Author's Money Tree

How to Grow a Bountiful Readership Organically

Kim Staflund

The Author's Money Tree
How to Grow a Bountiful Readership Organically

From the author who brought us

How to Publish a Bestselling Book touted as
"...exceptional, practical, detailed, comprehensive, and
thoroughly 'user friendly' from beginning to end."
by Midwest Book Review

and

Successful Selling Tips for Introverted Authors proclaimed
"...a 'must-have' for every author. Highly recommended."
by Wisconsin Bookwatch

Kim Staflund
Polished Publishing Group (PPG)

The Author's Holy Trinity of Profit (Book One)

The Author's Money Tree: How to Grow a Bountiful Readership Organically
Ebook ISBN: 978-1-988971-34-6
Paperback ISBN: 978-1-988971-35-3
© 2019 by Kim Staflund

🍁**PolishedPublishingGroup**

Due to the dynamic nature of the Internet, any website addresses mentioned within this book might have been changed or discontinued since its publication.

For writers:

"There is nothing to writing. All you do is sit down at a typewriter and bleed."
~Ernest Hemingway

The Author's Holy Trinity of Profit Trilogy

Action
The Author's Money Tree: How to Grow a Bountiful Readership Organically

Thought
The Author's Gold Rush: How to Harvest a Bountiful Crop Repeatedly

Faith
The Author's Magic Key: How to Stay on Track and Keep the Faith

TABLE OF CONTENTS

INTRODUCTION

It takes three full seasons to reap the *true* rewards of The Author's Money Tree: planting, growing, and harvesting. And it's well worth all the effort.

The Author's Money Tree Season #1: Planting

There are three effective ways to plant an abundance of seeds with your desired readership: productive blogging, prolific publishing, or (better yet) *both*. If you are strategic in the way you do these things, you'll be amazed by how quickly your sprouts begin to show.

That's the beauty of being a writer in this digital age of book publishing. Writing *is* selling in the online world. And keywords are the seeds you're planting to feed all your hungry readers at harvest time.

The Author's Money Tree Season #2: Growing

But those keywords will never be enough on their own. Each sprout needs to be fed and watered so it can grow, and this takes time and patience. Quality content is the fertilizer that breathes life into a sprout and helps it grow into a healthy sapling. Proper search engine optimization (SEO) is the mulch that prevents your sapling from being taken over by larger weeds.

You need a strong root system to grow a bountiful money tree that will bear fruit for you, year after year, and stand the test of time. This is crucial to your progressive success in future harvest seasons, and I'll show you exactly how to do it.

The Author's Money Tree Season #3: Harvesting

And now comes the fun part! Harvest time is when you reap the rewards of all your efforts.

In this section of the book, you'll meet some authors who are earning six-figure incomes from their readerships in their own harvest seasons. You'll learn some of the strategies they're using to harvest the same crops, over and over again, while planting new seeds each year.

Do you want to grow an abundant readership? This is a totally sustainable system that you can use successfully for fiction, non-fiction, and even poetry. Truth!

Even James Patterson Shakes The Author's Money Tree

Independent authors aren't the only ones shaking The Author's Money Tree in new ways. Even mainstream thriller author, James Patterson, has jumped on this band wagon with his BookShots line.

His reason for publishing books this way may be a bit different than the rest of us, as indicated in *The New York Times* article by Alexandra Alter titled "James Patterson Has a Big Plan for Small Books." After all, he doesn't need the money. But no matter who you are, the results are still the same.

> ...Mr. Patterson is after an even bigger audience. He wants to sell books to people who have abandoned reading for television, video games, movies and social media.

> So how do you sell books to somebody who doesn't normally read?

> Mr. Patterson's plan: make them shorter, cheaper, more plot-driven and more widely available.

> ...He aims to release two to four books a month through Little, Brown, his publisher. All of the titles will be shorter than 150 pages, the length of a novella. (Alter, 2016)

This is one of the greatest keys to success as an author in this day and age: prolific publishing. The single best way to sell books (and build a blog) is to utilize the power of search engines. Ping their algorithms by feeding them new content on a consistent basis. Do this, and they'll reward you by feeding you more traffic. It works the same for Kobo or Amazon's internal search engines as it does for Google, Baidu, Yahoo, or Bing.

But don't let high writing volumes scare you away. This is an entirely achievable plan—even for those of you still working full-time elsewhere while writing part-time on the side. You can still be *you* with the core aspects of your writing. Does this sound familiar?

> Some authors set aside a certain number of hours every day for writing, or a certain number of words. In short, a writing schedule.

> Then there's me. No writing for three or six months, then a flurry of activity where I forget to eat, sleep, bathe, change the cat's litter... I'm a walking stereotype. To assuage the guilt, I tell myself that my unconscious is hard at work. As Hemingway would say, long periods of thinking and short periods of writing. (LaRocca, 2019)

Well, in this book, I'm going to teach you how to take full advantage of "the writing flurries" when they happen. And, once you see the kind of results this program can bring, you may find those flurries increase naturally for you. That's what happened to me. In 2017 and 2018, I wrote and published 35 books and dozens of blog posts to go along with them. It's like the more I wrote, the more my creativity seemed to grow. But I refer you back to James Patterson's BookShots line again. Remember that he's writing *novellas*—not yesterday's idea of an "acceptable" full-length novel. And your blog posts? More good news: these no longer have to be 500+ words long to be effective, either. Even as few as 300 words can still constitute quality content in Google's eyes—so long as the post is set up properly. I'll show you how to blog productively yet efficiently in this book. You won't believe how easy this is!

This Program Can Work for Fiction, Non-Fiction, and Poetry

You could be in any room chatting with your family members, friends, or business colleagues. It doesn't matter where it is or who you're with. At some point during the conversation, a question of some sort almost always arises; what's the first thing everyone does? You each pull out your smartphone, iPad, or tablet and open the web browser to search for an answer to that question. We all have instant access to timely information at our fingertips now, and we're all *constantly* accessing it. Anik Singal, email marketer extraordinaire, says it best with this statement:

> Consider this: Twenty years ago if you wanted to learn something, you'd go to the library or bookstore and pick up a book. If there was new information on a

topic, it had to go through a long publication process - an average of 18 months! By the time that new information came out, it was often already outdated.

Today is very different.

We live in the Information Age. Basically, the greatest industry in the world today is the information industry. Those with access to information and the ability to distribute it the fastest are the ones who are poised to be our next millionaires and billionaires. (Singal, 2016)

Now let's take that a step further. As an author, it's not only about your ability to quickly distribute information to the masses that could potentially earn you thousands—even millions—of dollars; it's more about your ability to use that information to connect people together in meaningful ways. Intellectual property—information in the form of patented, trademarked, and copyrighted collections of ideas and concepts—can be priceless assets to the owners who know how to do this well.

In discussions with industry leaders like Seth Godin and Clay Hebert (among many others), it has become clear that we are in a Connection Economy. The connection economy rewards value created by building relationships and creating connections, rather than building assets by industrialism. This means the most valuable companies will connect buyer to seller, or consumer to content. If you don't buy that argument, consider these facts:

1. Uber is the largest "taxi" company - yet they own no vehicles and excel at connecting riders with drivers.

2. AirBnB is the largest provider of accommodations - yet they own no real estate.

3. Facebook is the largest media company - yet they create no content.

4. Crowdfunding businesses like Kickstarter and IndiGoGo [*sic*] are expected to surpass venture capital for funding in 2016 - yet they have no funds to invest.

Whereas it used to be sufficient to sell a product and receive revenues, customers now seek to connect with other like-minded individuals to get the most value in the long run. (Altman, 2015)

Authors can create these kinds of meaningful connections through books. Whether you're a fiction author dedicated to entertaining readers within a certain genre or a non-fiction subject matter expert (SME) who writes how-to or self-help materials, there are umpteen unique ways for you to bond with your readers while uniting them with additional people/resources that can enhance their reading experience. I'll show you some great ways to do this in chapter two, when we take a look at some easy blog post ideas together.

And poets? You have a choice: you can sell your work the way a fiction novelist does; or you can sell it the way a non-fiction SME does. There is a larger market for your poems than simply people who read poetry books for the sake of poetry. Just think about all the instances where poetry can be useful: in greeting cards; on motivational artwork for homes or offices; for obituaries; for special event speeches or presentations; et cetera. Poetry appeals to each reader's emotions in a different way than fiction and non-fiction does. But how you sell it is much the same, believe it or not.

How Do I Know This Works?

My shift in thinking began in around mid-to-late 2015. I had been in the book publishing business, in one capacity or another, for close to 25 years. I'd been publishing books under my own label, Polished Publishing Group (PPG), since November 2009. I knew how to produce a truly professional product for my authors, and I had ample experience to be able to teach them all the traditional book sales and marketing methods. I was a best selling author in my own right, and so were many of my authors. So, everything looked great on the surface.

But here was the reality: my company wasn't generating enough profit to allow me to leave my full-time sales job. My own royalties, and my best authors' royalties, weren't all that impressive. All these bestsellers were earning less than $500 per year in royalties. That was the hard truth. (Sound familiar? I'll bet it does.)

Burnout and Refocus Time

I was burning out. I could no longer maintain my pace of 50+ hours of corporate sales coupled with another 20+ hours of book publishing, sales, and marketing every week. Especially if there was no end in sight to all this work—no definite increase in profits to show me I was on the right track. I felt discouraged. I felt like I was failing my authors, never mind myself.

So, do you want to know what I did? I quit my full-time job, and I scaled back the publishing work for a little while. There was something I had wanted to do since my early twenties that I allowed myself to do in my forties. I embarked on my very own "Eat, Pray, Love" working holiday in Asia and taught English in Bangkok, Thailand, in 2016. What a blessing this experience was! I was blessed not only by all the people I met and all the life lessons I learned, but also by my renewed sense of purpose when I returned home.

If you're feeling burned out in any way, I recommend you do something like this for yourself. Walk away from your work for a while. Have fun! Eat! Pray! Love! Then, once you're fully rejuvenated, get back to work. You'll be so much more productive if you do. And you may just find the answers to your questions that had eluded you for so long. That's what happened to me.

Sell More Earn More in the United Kingdom

I didn't go back to a "real job" straightaway because I wanted to turn off the corporate noise for a while and *really* focus on my craft. I found four personal investors to help me cover my expenses while I focused. In early 2017, I started studying and learning all about email marketing. I also Googled things like "successful authors" and "profitable publishing" to figure out how to take things to the next level and start making some *real* money publishing books.

The first clue came to me in the form of a *Forbes* article, titled "Amazon Pays $450,000 A Year To This Self-Published Writer," written about an independent author in the United Kingdom named Mark Dawson. I was impressed but skeptical. I figured maybe he was an anomaly. So, I kept reading and searching for more "realistic" examples of success.

Sell More Earn More in the United States

In May of 2017, I spoke at a writers' conference in Columbia, Missouri. Because I only presented two break-out sessions of my own, I had the opportunity to attend many other people's sessions that weekend. One of the most memorable sessions for me was Liz Schulte's break-out session. This American was one of only a handful of independent authors who were allowed to join her local traditional writers' guild. Why? Because of her *proven* sales success. She was already earning a six-figure annual royalty in her second year of self-publishing.

WHAT??!!

Now it wasn't just some seemingly "faraway fictional character" speaking to me about his success from a *Forbes* magazine article. This was a real person standing in front of me, telling me that she was doing many of the same things Mark Dawson was doing. And she was seeing similar results. Now I knew I was onto something big!

I went for a glass of wine with Liz that evening, and I soaked in all her knowledge. I also asked her to write a guest post for the PPG Publisher's Blog and she willingly obliged despite how busy she is. Thank you, Liz.

Sell More Earn More in Australia

Determined to meet even more authors like Mark and Liz, I posted a question on Quora asking authors to share their success stories with me. I received a somewhat cheeky reply from an Aussie, named Timothy Ellis, who said he wasn't sure if I would consider him a success or not because he only sells around 3,000 books per month after two years as a self-publisher.

WHAT??!!

How? Give me your success formula! Show me your stats!

Lucky for me, he obliged. Timothy Ellis willingly shared his success formula in another guest post on the PPG Publisher's Blog. Thank you, Timothy.

Sell More Earn More in Canada … and All Over the World!

Long story short, since that time, I've been a student of many more successful authors who are following similar patterns as the above three are. I've also learned all kinds of effective tools authors can use to improve their ranking on various search engines. In fact, I've studied and put into practice everything I've learned to see some success of my own over the past two years.

Here's the best part: I picked up a "real job" again about a year ago. And even with this full-time work taking up much of my time during the week, I'm still seeing some real progress with both my blog and my own personal book sales. So, that tells you that *you* can do the same. You don't have to quit your job and focus on writing and publishing alone in order to see success with this program. You can easily maintain both … until you don't have to do both anymore.

Some authors begin to see significant results after only one or two years. For Joanna Penn, it took five years to transition to being a full-time writer. It took another four to earn a six-figure income. Still, it was well worth the time and effort as she now earns a *multi* six-figure income as an author and blogger. I'll tell you more about her, and why she's become one of my greatest mentors from afar, in the last chapter of this book. I hope to some day meet her in person.

Everyone's journey with this will be a little bit different. But I'm going to share the kinds of activities that will get you well on your way to success—the kind of success you may not have thought was possible for an author before. Whether you're self-published or traditionally published—and whether you're selling fiction, non-fiction, or poetry—this program can benefit you if you follow it closely. That much I'm sure of.

THE AUTHOR'S MONEY TREE SEASON #1: PLANTING

Every day, people are searching for books like yours online. They perform those searches by typing various words and phrases (known as keywords) into search engines like Google and online bookstores like Amazon and Kobo. The more keywords you can associate with your book(s), and the higher your ranking grows on each of these websites, the better your chance of being found by the people searching for your topic matter.

The Power of Google in Helping You Sell Books

We'll start this book with a closer look at Google itself. This search engine powers over 73% of all Internet searches according to this December 2018 NetMarketShare report: https://netmarketshare.com/search-engine-market-share.aspx. The same report shows China's Baidu as second in line at almost 13%; so, that tells you the power of Google in helping you to sell more books. All you need now is some guidance regarding how to optimize your search engine ranking on Google, for all your major keywords, so your desired readers can easily find you.

For starters, let's call on the expert crew at Moz to explain what exactly search engine optimization (SEO) is. I found a concise description of the term in this aptly-titled article "What is SEO?" from the company's SEO Learning Centre:

> Search engine optimization (SEO) is the practice of increasing the quantity and quality of traffic to your website through organic search engine results. (MOZ, n.d.)

What constitutes *quality* traffic? It is relevant visitors to your website—people who are looking for exactly the types of books and information that you offer. What is an *organic* search engine result? It is a natural search result—one that you didn't pay for via online advertising methods such as pay-per-click (PPC) advertising. The more clickable links that direct quality traffic to a website, that show up in the top five or 10 organic search results (relative to an unlimited number of keyword searches), the more potential customers will likely visit that website. If that website happens to be your blog or your book's webpage on an ecommerce site, this will improve your readership (fan base) and help you build your name as a reputable author within your genre. And, make no mistake about it, your reputation is an important ranking factor in Google's eyes.

You see, Google was founded in September of 1998 with the sole purpose of creating a useful search experience for people to navigate through the ever-growing world wide web, so they could easily find whatever specific information they were looking for online. It was as simple as that, and Google's user base grew quickly because of it.

Unfortunately, some sneaky hackers figured out the background coding Google was using to index search results and determine which websites would show up at the top. These hackers used this knowledge to rank their own websites higher than anyone else's—whether their content was relevant to the searches being done or not. One of the techniques early hackers used is called "keyword stuffing" in which they would load their webpages full of high-ranking keywords or numbers (most of them hidden in the background) to manipulate their ranking and put them on top. The Google team caught wind of this and the first of many updates was launched—to render keyword stuffing useless and stop these types of hackers and spammers in their tracks. After all, if Google wanted to keep its user base happy, it had to keep its search results clean, relevant, and helpful.

That is the essence of every new update to this day. Google wants to keep its user base happy through these three search quality factors: expertise, authority, trust (EAT). If you maintain a consistent reputation of providing relevant and helpful content that shows your expertise, authority, and trustworthiness within your genre, you'll rank higher and higher in Google's search results over time. So, make sure you EAT regularly to keep your website ranking healthy!

Here's something else I recently read in Adam Clarke's book titled *SEO 2018: Learn Search Engine Optimization With Smart Internet Marketing Strategies* that made me smile:

> Google have been outspoken about readability as an important consideration for webmasters. Google's former head of web spam, Matt Cutts, publicly stated that poorly researched and misspelled content will rank poorly, and clarity should be your focus. And by readability, this means not just avoiding spelling mistakes, but making your content readable for the widest possible audience, with simple language and sentence structures.

> ...The Searchmetrics rankings report discovered sites appearing in the top 10 showed an average Flesch reading score of 76.00—content that is fairly easy to read for 13-15 year old students and up.

> ...By encouraging search results to have content readable to a wide audience, Google maximise their

advertising revenues. If Google were to encourage complicated results that mostly appeal to a smaller demographic, such as post-graduates, it would lower Google's general appeal and their market share. (Clarke, 2018)

This statement makes me smile not only because it encourages editing, but also because it matches my own business philosophies that drive how I write my blog entries and books, and how I run my book publishing company as a whole. I've always maintained that when people are unable to explain their topic matter to others in layman's terms with ease, they're either hiding something or they don't fully understand it themselves. I'd rather be clear and helpful. I was glad to learn the team at Google sees it the same way. Clearly, I'm in good company in this regard.

It All Starts with a Book and a Blog

If you have published (or plan to publish) a book, you will need a website to promote it online. That's your starting point. You don't need anything fancy or expensive; a simple blog will do. If you haven't already done so, you can create one for yourself free of charge using WordPress. Just follow their user-friendly instructions along with the instructions I give you in this book.

I'm recommending WordPress here because it is the platform I use for my own blog, and I'm familiar with its plug-ins. But much of what I'm recommending here can be done without the use of WordPress plug-ins; so, if you're using a different platform, such as Blogger, that's fine. You can make that work just as well.

Why exactly do you need a blog? Think of your blog as the primary web address where you can promote *everything* related to your authorship: books (e.g., audiobooks, ebooks, paperbacks, hardcovers); upcoming book signings/speaking events; videos; podcasts; photography or sketches; questions and answers for your fans; et cetera. It's important to make your content-rich site easy for users to find and navigate because that also makes it easier for Google's search engine spiders (also sometimes referred to as web crawlers) to find and index. I'll show you exactly how to do that in chapters one and two.

Why is a Blog Better for Authors than a Regular Website?

I'll begin by clarifying that a blog *is* a type of website. Basically, anything you visit online that has its own URL (e.g., web address, domain name) is a website.

To use a familiar analogy, they're all fruit. But you can think of traditional, static websites as apples. And you can consider blogs to be oranges. One of these fruits is much juicier than the other in terms of helping you to improve your SEO and get noticed by more readers online. And your sole purpose in having any type of online presence is to do just that: attract a larger readership to your book(s).

Website vs. Blog: Apple vs. Orange

As mentioned above, a traditional website is static in that once you create it, it just stays the same and sits there online waiting for people to view it. But a blog is dynamic. This means its content is always being updated. If you're blogging correctly, you're adding new content to your blog at least three times per week. And this is important to SEO. Search engines love new content. They eat it up! The more relevant and helpful new content you give them to share with their users, the more they'll reward you by placing you higher and higher in their ranking.

A traditional website is meant to provide basic information about you. What are your books about? Where can you be contacted? But a blog provides an expanded view of your author business as a whole. A blog is where you can share your thoughts, opinions, experiences, event calendars, and book excerpts in more meaningful ways.

Blogs allow for reader engagement in the form of the comments section at the bottom of each post. Websites don't have this ability. If you can get your readers to engage with you in this way, then you know you're having an impact with them. That's important.

Website vs. Blog: Summary

Websites are static, contain basic information, and don't allow for reader engagement. A website is limited in its ability to improve your SEO.

Blogs are dynamic, provide your readers with an expanded view, and allow reader engagement in the form of comments. Since search engines love new content, blogs are the single best way for you to improve your SEO online. But if you truly want each blog entry to be indexed by search engines like Google, then you'll have to set them up a certain way and ensure they have an optimal Flesch Reading Ease Score (FRES). We'll discuss this in more detail in chapter two.

Keywords are the Seeds That Will Grow Your Readership

You will want to blog about various aspects of your authorship at least three times per week, if not more. And you'll want each individual blog post to have its own focused keyword. Why? A keyword is like a seed that, when planted in fertile soil, will germinate and multiply itself repeatedly until it becomes countless more seeds of the same variety. Thus, the more seeds you plant and grow, the larger your harvest will be.

Keyword Research is Crucial to Your Success

The keywords you include within each individual blog post (and, for the independent authors reading this, within all your book descriptions) are crucial to your success. That's why keyword research is possibly the most important aspect of SEO. Because if you do all the things I recommend in this book and you obtain a high ranking for the *wrong* keywords, you won't attract that *quality* traffic you're after—those relevant visitors who are looking for your type of books. Or, worse yet, if you "put all your eggs into one basket," as it were, by using only a few overly competitive keywords on your website, you may not rank at all against the more popular and established authors' websites. It's a balancing act of adding enough different keywords to your blog entries—common and unique keywords, broad match and exact match keywords—and then monitoring them daily to "sort the wheat from the chaff," so to speak. Luckily, there are some useful online tools available to help you do just that.

How to Know Which Keywords Will Send Quality Traffic to Your Website

If you want to successfully sell books online using SEO, you need to take some time to think things through. You need to sit down and create a list of all the possible keywords that relate to the genre of books you're promoting online. Once you come up with a large enough list (e.g., 3 posts per week times 52 weeks per year equals 156 keywords), you can test all those keywords using actual search traffic data to determine which ones will be most useful for you (e.g., which ones will bring you the quality traffic you desire that has the best chance of turning into a book sale and new loyal reader for you).

Google Analytics (https://www.google.com/analytics/#?modal_active=none) is a free tool that helps you monitor your performance on search engines by tracking and reporting on your current website traffic. It can give you a pretty clear picture of where your visitors are coming from in terms of both geographic regions and sources (e.g., other websites that are redirecting this traffic to you) so you can keep track of your backlinks.

The Google AdWords Keyword Planner (https://adwords.google.com/intl/en_ca/start/#?modal_active=none) is another useful resource that you must pay to use either by running a pay-per-click (PPC) advertising campaign or by paying a monthly user fee. The keyword planner allows you to see, in real time, which of your keywords are being searched online versus which ones aren't coming up at all—so you can trash the useless ones from your list rather than adding them to your blog posts or PPC campaigns. Very useful information.

How to "Borrow" Keyword Research from Other High-Ranking Authors in Your Genre

But all that research takes time, doesn't it? Luckily, there is another free and easy resource called the SEOBook Keyword Analyzer (http://tools.seobook.com/general/keyword-density/) that will allow you to analyze the websites of other bestselling authors within your genre to determine which top keywords they're each currently using to obtain such a high ranking. When you visit the SEOBook Keyword Analyzer website, you'll see it's as simple as typing each author's web address into the box, one at a time, and then clicking on the submit button. Within seconds, a detailed list of their title page, meta keywords, and meta descriptions will appear before your eyes. You can use this data as research for your own blog's keywords.

Different Types of Keywords Bring Different Results

There's more to it than simply adding as many keywords to your campaign as you can think of that prospective readers may use to find you and your book. Different types of keywords will bring different results. For example:

- **Broad Match Keywords:** This is the default type of keyword, and it looks like this: financial planning (or this: +financial +planning). A keyword like this can trigger any number of different search results such as financial reporting, financial advisor salary, planning ahead, financial news, planning and development, and the list goes on.
- **Phrase Match Keywords:** If you put quotes around the keyword ("financial planning"), then it will trigger search results that contain that precise phrase in them such as financial planning books, financial

planning standards council, financial planning and analysis, financial planning courses, et cetera.

- **Exact Match Keywords:** If you want to trigger ads for the exact phrase *only*, then you must put brackets around it like this: [financial planning].
- **Negative Keywords:** If you ever run a pay-per-click (PPC) advertising campaign to help you sell more books, you will want to add negative keywords to that campaign to prevent yourself being charged for the clicks you don't really want. For example, maybe you've written an ebook about financial planning. If your goal is to direct people to that ebook alone, you may want to add -paperback and -magazine (with a minus sign in front of the word) to your negative keywords list. That way, you'll avoid the readers who are searching for paperbacks and magazines about financial planning.

Here's some more tried and true advice from Google Certified Professional and *SEO 2018* author Adam Clarke:

> When choosing keywords, you need a balance between keywords with a high level of accuracy, such as exact match keywords, and keywords with a larger amount of reach, such as phrase match or broad match modified keywords. (Clarke, 2018)

Balance is the key when you're planting your seeds each week. Patience will help you, too, because some of those seeds are bound to grow faster than others. That's just life.

What's the Difference Between Tags and Keywords?

Tags and keywords both help people to find information on your blog. But there are key differences between the two that are important to understand.

You may assume, as I once did, that the tags you attach to each blog post are helping your SEO on *external* search engines like Google. But those tags are simply labels that help your blog readers find information *within* your blog. For example, if you're a dietitian, you may want to assign the label "vegan protein" to all the posts you write about hemp hearts, quinoa, brown rice, et cetera. That way, all those articles will come up when readers search for vegan protein recommendations on your blog.

What Search Engines are Looking For

If you want external search engines to find each of those posts, you must assign a specific *keyword* to each post. You can do this quite easily using a plug-in like Yoast SEO WordPress to guide you on how to set up each blog post in an SEO-friendly way. How you write each post is important. It can still be effective, from an SEO standpoint, at only 300 words in length. But there are certain things you must do to ensure the search engine crawlers know exactly which keyword you want attached to that post. We'll talk about those things in chapter two.

THE AUTHOR'S MONEY TREE SEASON #2: GROWING

In chapter one, you researched and found the perfect seeds that will help you grow your readership over time. You learned how to plant them, one by one, in fertile soil. Now you'll learn how to add fertilizer and mulch to give your crop every possible chance to grow tall and strong.

10 Easy Ways to Fertilize and Insulate Your Crop

There are 10 simple things authors can do to improve your Google ranking. Do *some* of these things on a regular basis, and you'll begin to see an increase in your blog traffic which will most likely result in some extra book sales for you. Do *all* these things on a consistent basis, and the result should be a significant increase to your blog traffic, readership, *and* book sales at harvest time. The key to your success is consistency of purpose.

I mentioned earlier that Google wants to keep its user base happy through these three important search quality factors: expertise, authority, trust (EAT). You prove your expertise online by means of digital (downloadable) books and other relevant information that is published regularly and often on ecommerce sites such as Amazon and Kobo, your own blog, and other appropriate websites. Your authority is eventually proven by the number of book reviews, backlinks, plus social media followers, likes, and shares that you accumulate over time due to these publishing activities. In a search engine's eyes, if your books have more legitimate reviews than other authors' books within the same genre, your social media sites have more followers, and each of your webpages (e.g., each individual post on your blog site, each individual book on Amazon or Kobo, et cetera) have more click-throughs, then you must have more authority than the other authors have. As a result, you'll rank higher than they do. It's as simple as that, and it's all based on algorithms.

1. Publish relevant content on a consistent basis:

    Blogging is one of the best ways for you to stay engaged with your current and prospective readership; and, the more often you post something new online, the more points Google will award to your blog site thus improving its SEO. But you should know that Google is far from being the only search engine that rewards new content. Amazon and Kobo do, too. Want to *dramatically* increase your SEO over the next year? Start posting relevant and helpful content on a consistent basis that pleases *all* these search engines. That's what many of today's most successful independent authors are doing. I already mentioned a few of them in this book's introduction. I'll introduce you to a few more in the final chapter of this book. Success leaves clues … just do what they do, and you'll see.

2. Build a high number of relevant backlinks to your website:

    What is a backlink? It is a clickable hyperlink from someone else's website that directs people back to your website.

    Legitimate book reviews, guest blogging, and content syndication can be used to increase the number of relevant backlinks to your blog site. This, too, is worthy of a higher ranking in Google's eyes thus improving your

SEO. It expands the reach of each seed you plant.

3. Protect and improve your SEO with REL=CANONICAL and META NOINDEX tags:

While guest blogging and content syndication are both fantastic ways to improve your website's SEO, they can also cause duplicate content issues if too much of the same copy is being reused on different sites without due care. Why? Because search engine algorithms can detect copied/reused content—and copied/reused content is a no-no in the online world, which will be discussed in more detail a bit later. For now, I'll say that this is where implementing rel=canonical and meta noindex HTML tags can come in handy:

"The rel=canonical element, often called the "canonical link", is an HTML element that helps webmasters prevent duplicate content issues. It does this by specifying the "canonical URL", the "preferred" version of a web page. Using it well improves a site's SEO." (Yoast, 2018)

The rel=canonical tag must be added to the header section of whichever webpage will be redirecting back to the URL that contains original content. The HTML coding being added to that header will look something like this: <link rel="canonical" href="http://originalcontentlink.com/">.

"What this does is "merge" the two pages into one from a search engine's perspective. It's a "soft redirect", without redirecting the user. Links to both URLs now count for the single canonical version of the URL." (Yoast, 2018)

Yoast also has a WordPress plug-in that can be used to improve your blog's SEO by helping you to remove certain pages from search engine indexes altogether. Using a plug-in is an easier way for newbies to utilize HTML elements like these because they don't have to edit their website headers themselves. The plug-in does everything for them.

Which pages might you want to add meta noindex tags to? Possibly any syndicated content you posted from someone else's online publication to "beef up" your own content. You can learn more about the Yoast plug-in that can help you do this here: https://kb.yoast.com/kb/how-do-i-noindex-urls/#single.

4. Attract regular click-through traffic to your website:

    It stands to reason that the more content you post, the more backlinks that redirect to your site, and the higher your SEO ranking grows, then the more traffic will find its way to your website and click on it. You want these people to stay there as long as possible. If they only click once and then leave, that's called a bounce; but, if they click on a few different pages and stay there for a while to read things over, that's called a click-through. A high bounce rate may affect your SEO negatively while you'll garner more SEO points via an increased click-through rate—all the more reason to ensure your website contains relative and enticing content people will want to stay and view.

5. Encourage more social media activity and shares (e.g., Facebook, Twitter, LinkedIn, and YouTube):

   I dedicated an entire book, titled *Successful Selling Tips for Introverted Authors*, to teaching authors how to utilize social media marketing as part of your online sales strategy. Did you know social media activity is one of the things Google rewards that can help to improve your SEO? Well, it *is*. And certain social media sites will earn you more points than others, so I've learned. For example, did you know YouTube is owned by Google? Now that you know this, you may be more inclined to start posting video content on a regular basis.

6. Make sure your website is mobile-friendly:

   On March 26, 2018, Google went live with its new Mobile-First Index which you can find more information about here: https://developers.google.com/search/mobile-sites/mobile-first-indexing. According to Google, "Mobile-first indexing means Google will predominantly use the mobile version of the content for indexing and ranking. Historically, the index primarily used the desktop version of a page's content when evaluating the relevance of a page to a user's query. Since the majority of users now access Google via a mobile device, the index will primarily use the mobile version of a page's content going forward. We aren't creating a separate mobile-first index. We continue to use only one index." This is why I not only use WordPress for my blog but also for my company's primary website now: https://polishedpublishinggroup.com/. WordPress sites are mobile-friendly. In fact, they look great on *all* devices.

7. Protect your website's security with SSL security certificates:

   In this new world of WikiLeaks and expert hackers with the ability to break into websites and steal other people's private information, Google has become a strong advocate of website encryption. In fact, Google decided to add SSL security certificates to its list of top-ranking factors back in 2014. By purchasing such a certificate, you're providing an extra level of security to anyone who fills in an online form (e.g., a contact form, blog registration form, order form) on your website. This provides them with a direct connection to your server that no one else can eavesdrop on. Once you add an SSL security certificate to your website, you'll notice that your URL (Uniform Resource Locator, also called a web address) starts with HTTPS: rather than the standard HTTP: and has a green padlock image beside it. More and more, Google is looking for that padlock and will reward you points for having it. Luckily, WordPress sites are easily secured.

8. Include attractive images and easy-to-read fonts in your website's main content area to encourage more time on the site:

   As mentioned earlier, making your site easy for users to find and navigate also makes it easier for Google's search engine spiders to find and index; so, keep your users in mind when designing your blog site, particularly your home page. Make your blog attractive by including relevant, clickable images (perhaps your book covers with links to the ecommerce sites where they can be purchased). According to Adam Clarke, images and larger, more readable fonts can lead to a higher engagement with your site which will result in a higher click-through rate and a lower bounce rate thus boosting your Google ranking.

9. Increase Pinterest activity:

    Until I read Adam's book, I wouldn't have given that much thought to Pinterest; but, apparently, engagement with this "visual social media" website is listed as one of the top things Google is giving points for these days. If the target readership for your books is women, then set up a free Pinterest account for yourself because this site has an 80% female user base according to this article on Infront Webworks: https://www.infront.com/blog/the-infront-blog/what-is-pinterest-and-how-does-it-work. Upload images of your book covers (these uploads are known as "pins" on Pinterest) along with associated links to more information about each book on your blog. If you write on non-fiction lifestyle topics—gardening, cooking, fashion, and decorating to name only a few—then Pinterest may be an especially great promotional tool for you. You can also share your How-To YouTube videos here to further promote your books.

10. Answer industry-related questions on your blog to encourage featured snippets inclusion:

    To increase your chances of having a featured snippet of your writing included in Google searches, some of your blog posts should be formatted as detailed answers to the most commonly asked questions within your genre; and the titles of these blog posts should be formatted as the questions themselves. Believe me, your work may be well-rewarded for doing so.

What is a featured snippet? Basically, whenever you do any kind of search on Google and then click enter to bring up the results, you'll notice there are two or three listings at the very top that have the word "Ad" inside a little box to the left of their website links. And, if your search phrase was formed as a question, you may also see a large box filled with an answer to your question which is known as a featured snippet. These are both forms of Google AdWords, but one is paid for with your money while the other is paid for with your time and clever writing skills. You can think of a featured snippet as an "earned placement" for high-ranking webpages that take the time to answer common questions, relevant to their industries (or, in the case of authors, their genres), in a clear and direct way. Here's a great article explaining more about how featured snippets work: https://searchengineland.com/get-featured-snippets-site-224959.

I think this is an interesting concept in a lot of ways. First of all, it can really get one's creative juices flowing in terms of coming up with new content ideas for this week's blog posts. If you write fictional vampire novels, then you may want to write a few different blog posts such as: Why do vampires drink blood? Why do vampires sleep in coffins? Why do vampires have no reflection? Why do vampires dislike garlic? These kinds of posts will provide something a little fun and different for your regular readership, outside of your regular posts about new characters and plots in your upcoming books. Better yet, they may just earn you a featured snippet which attracts a whole new level of traffic to your blog and books.

If you write non-fiction health and fitness guides, then you may want to write a few blog entries that answer these common questions: What is the best way to lose fat fast? Will I get bigger muscles from weight lifting? How do I get a flat stomach? What is my target heart rate? Whatever questions you can think of that seem to come up repeatedly in your industry, use them as the titles of a few of your blog entries each month, then answer each question in a clear and direct Google-friendly way.

And poets? What if you answered some of these types of questions for us: What are the different types of poetry? What are the elements of a haiku? How do I write a limerick? These are just a few ideas. You get the picture. Just remember this when you're writing: keep that Searchmetrics rankings report in mind that showed an average Flesch reading score of 76.00 in the websites that ranked in the top 10 Google searches for their industries. Write for that audience for the best possible SEO results.

So, now you have a list of 10 important Google ranking factors that can help you to significantly increase the readership of your blog and books over time. To summarize this chapter, I want to share another sentence from Adam

Clarke's book that I believe recaps everything we've discussed regarding the simple essence of SEO and keywords:

> Focus on improving the quality of your site, provide good mobile support, earn good quality backlinks, improve your security for users and increase the social media activity associated with your site. (Clarke, 2018)

If you consistently focus on all these things, you will enjoy a higher search engine ranking over time. And you know what a high ranking means, right? A bountiful harvest later!

SEO-Friendly Flesch Reading Ease Score (FRES)

Yesterday's advice regarding writing the most SEO-friendly blog posts was simple. Make sure your post is genuinely helpful and contains at least 500 words. Within those 500 words, your main keyword should be repeated at least 10 times. By doing that, search engines like Google should be able to easily find and index the blog entry based on that keyword.

As mentioned earlier, today's advice is a little bit different. According to *SEO 2018* author Adam Clarke and Yoast: SEO for Everyone, writing each blog post with an SEO-friendly Flesch Reading Ease Score (FRES) is crucial to your SEO success.

Why I Now Use the Free Yoast SEO WordPress Plug-In

In a nutshell, the free Yoast SEO WordPress plug-in helps me to write blog posts that Google will approve and index. That's why I use it. Because Google is the greatest link between me and my desired reader base.

As I begin writing each and every blog post, the Yoast plug-in continually gives me little notices. It lets me know whether my content is SEO-friendly in various ways. It tells me if my FRES is within the acceptable 60.0 to 70.0 readability range. If not, it will show me which sentences need to be adjusted to improve that score.

Your Blog Posts Can Be 300+ Words Long

So long as your writing style matches Google's desired FRES score, your post can be 300+ words long. Yoast also has a different way of viewing keywords. Rather than repeating your top keyword at least twice within every 100 words, Yoast wants to see it right upfront. If you include that keyword in your slug (the URL for the blog entry), at least one or more of your headings, *and* within your first paragraph, Yoast will usually give you a good SEO score. It's also great to attach the keyword to an image on your blog post, too. That way, Google will certainly understand which keyword you want the post indexed under. Make sense?

There are additional things you can do to improve your blog post's SEO. Including internal links to past blog posts and external links to other relevant information will also help. The more posts you write that Yoast awards a good readability and SEO score to, the higher up your blog will land in Google's search engine ranking under several different keywords.

10 Easy Author Blog Post Ideas

Writing regular blog posts, at least three times per week, is a great way for you to increase your online exposure and search engine ranking. These 10 author blog post ideas will inspire you to write lots!

5 Author Blog Post Ideas About You and Your Books

1. It's fairly easy to write about yourself and what inspired you to start writing at all. Make some of your 156 posts about you. Let your readers get to know you better. Maybe that will include sharing a copy of the very first story or poem you ever wrote. For example, here's my first poem in the Western Producer:

I wrote that poem when I was 11 years old; it was published a few months later, just after I turned 12. My brother found it for me in the newspaper archives years later and it put a huge smile on my face to read it once again as an adult.

2. Include excerpts from your upcoming books to create a buzz around them before they're officially published. You've probably noticed I include plenty of book excerpts in the Coming Soon to PPG! category of my blog. If you're

publishing a new book at least every four to six weeks like I do, this will take care of eight or nine of your blog posts for the year.

3. What inspires you? Share the occasional inspirational quote and talk about why it speaks to your heart.

4. What is your creative process? Are you a plotter or a pantser? Share your writing tips and strategies with your readers. Invite them to share theirs in the comments section below.

5. Do you ever attend any writer's retreats or conferences in your area? Post about your experiences, the people you've met, and the impact they've had on you and your writing.

5 Author Blog Post Ideas About Other People or Places

6. Highlight other authors within your genre whose books inspired you in some way. Review their books on your blog and include the Amazon affiliate links (see "What Does it Mean to Monetize Your Blog?" for details) to those books within each blog post. If people purchase one of their books along with one of yours, that could help your Amazon ranking through association.

7. Did you hire any illustrators, graphic designers, or other professionals to help you produce a quality book? Why not dedicate some of your posts to writing biographies about them and their important contributions? Better yet, ask them to guest post on your blog. (Remember what you read earlier about this world's "connection economy" and how to best utilize it.)

8. Read the industry news and post your opinions about hot topics on your blog. What pleases you about these current

events? What displeases you? Why? Start a discussion and invite your subscribers to post their own comments below.

9. What geographic regions do your characters work or live in (for fiction or poetry), or what region are *you* currently writing in/about (for non-fiction)? Some of your posts can be geography lessons about these locations. Be sure to include pictures or videos for extra impact.

10. Search Quora for industry-related questions. Answer those questions for people on your own blog.

What Does it Mean to Monetize Your Blog?

When authors think about ways they can earn money from their writing, most think in terms of royalties from book sales. But you can also monetize your blog. The larger your blog's subscriber list grows, the more this will work to your advantage.

When you "monetize your blog," you are converting it into a source of income. Passive income. It works much the same way as book royalties do. You only have to write a book once. If people are still buying that book years after you first published it, those royalties are money earned without any additional effort on your part. Your blog posts can generate cash flow for years to come, too. It all depends on how you set up your blog.

If you are new to blogging and have only written a few posts up to now, there is one thing you can do immediately to monetize your blog. If you've been blogging for quite a while now, and you already have a pretty solid subscriber base, there are additional things you can do.

Set up an Affiliate Account Through Amazon Associates

In my opinion, the best affiliate marketing program for blogs is Amazon Associates. Why? In a word: choices. Through this program, you can sell everything and anything Amazon has to offer through your blog—not only books. You do this by creating personalized HTML links to the Amazon products of your choice through your Amazon Associates account. Then you post those links into the background coding of your website. Whenever someone visits your blog, clicks on those links, and makes a purchase through them on Amazon, you'll be paid an affiliate commission.

Set Up a Google AdSense Account

Once you've been blogging for a while and have daily traffic visiting your blog, you can apply for a Google AdSense account. What is that? Well, I mentioned pay-per-click (PPC) advertising earlier in this book. PPC is a "pay as you go" Internet advertising model people use to direct traffic to their websites. Advertisers pay only when their ads are clicked. For the campaigns that are run through Google Ads, PPC ads can show up in several places online—not only on the search engine itself. In fact, those ads can even show up on *your* blog through the Google AdSense program.

It takes a couple weeks from the time you submit your website to Google AdSense for consideration to the time they approve it. Once approved, Google will send you a unique HTML code. You can add it to any one or more pages of your website. I personally add it to the bottom of each and every one of my blog posts. That way, PPC ads appear in there that match best with the keyword and topic matter associated with each of those pages. You can do the same. Then any time someone visits your page and clicks on any of those PPC ads, you will earn a portion of Google's PPC profits from it. This is an easy way for you to earn some extra passive income from your blog.

The Value of Guest Blogging

Blogging, in general, is so important for authors. It can help you to develop and maintain an online presence which, in this day and age, is crucial to your commercial success. You can use your own and other people's blogs to share sample chapters of upcoming books as a form of advertising, and as an opportunity to receive feedback from others before publishing it. The idea of receiving feedback on your work may seem frightening at first, but constructive criticism can be so valuable to you in ways you've never thought of before. For example, many of today's top independent authors use their subscribers as "beta testers" prior to publishing—to garner useful assessments as to whether certain aspects of the writing can be improved in some way before it is released for mass public consumption. When you think of it as a form of market testing like these authors do, suddenly the feedback becomes less personal and more helpful.

Organically improving one's SEO via blogging can be a slow process—especially when you're doing it alone—because it requires a regular, consistent effort on your part to produce at least three posts per week. Most people want faster results. Luckily, there are ways you can increase the speed of this process by partnering with other people and their blogs/websites.

The value of networking with others cannot be stressed enough. Not only can it help you produce extra content for your blog, it can also create valuable backlinks to your blog from other high-ranking websites. You can learn so much from other authors and bloggers, and they can learn from you. The benefits are many as we'll discuss throughout this chapter.

When You Guest Post on Someone Else's Blog

Providing original content for someone else's blog can help you to achieve three key goals: one, it can help you to position yourself as an authority of your particular topic matter to an extended audience; two, it can bring more exposure to your own blog which may help to increase your subscriber base; and three, it can create backlinks to your blog from the webpages you are guest posting on. You'll want to partner with bloggers who post regular content that is similar to yours for an audience who will be interested in your topic matter. You'll also want to make sure the blog has a pretty strong subscriber base of its own. Better yet if the bloggers you're partnering with are active on social media, so you know they're promoting all their blog posts on a consistent basis. All these things will help to improve your chances of online success.

How do you find guest posting opportunities? Start with Google. In the search results box, type in a keyword related to your industry followed by any of the following keywords: guest posting opportunities; accepting guest posts; submit a guest post; guest post. You can also do similar searches on social media sites such as Twitter or Facebook to find guest posting opportunities for yourself there.

Before you contact any other bloggers to request a guest posting opportunity with them, you'll want to read through some of their blogs' archives and categories to get a sense of what type of topic matter is being covered. Doing so will help you to adjust your proposed content to better match what they're looking for in terms of audience (beginner, intermediate, advanced), format (some prefer point-form posts while others want longer paragraphs), graphics (if they include images with their posts then you should do the same), and word count (300 words? 500 words? more?) prior to contacting them. This will increase your chances of being accepted for inclusion on their blogs.

Your pitch letter should include a little bit of information about you as an author, what sorts of topic matter you cover in your books and your blog, and why it's such a great fit for their audience. If you have any success stories to share in terms of bestselling status of any of your books or high view/share statistics for any of your past blog posts, then share this information in your letter, too. Let other bloggers know that a partnership with you will be mutually beneficial.

Remember to keep the needs of your audience in mind ahead of your own when you're writing a guest post. What I mean by this is that the post, itself, should never be purely an advertisement for your own book or business. You can save that type of information for your author bio at the end. The post should be useful information that will help the audience in some way, whether it's to entertain them by providing an excerpt to an upcoming fictional novel or inform them with some other type of helpful guidance.

On the PPG Publisher's Blog, I allow my guest posters to include links to their latest books within their posts. I'm always looking for additional value for my subscribers (up and above the information I already provide to them) in the form of genuinely helpful tips/advice that will support them in various aspects of their book writing, publishing, sales, and marketing careers. I like to keep the flow of information open and easy for everyone involved, so there aren't any hard and fast deadlines to meet nor any specific word counts that must be met. Allowing guest posters to highlight their own books on my blog is, I believe, not only for *their* benefit (my way of thanking them for the post) but also for the benefit of my subscribers. If the subscribers are interested in picking up a book that is related to the topic matter they're enjoying, then why should they have to go searching for that book elsewhere? I want to have a link to it available right there in the content so it's easy for them to find, click, and buy. That helps everyone.

When Someone Else Guest Posts on Your Blog

The most obvious benefit to having someone else guest post relevant, original content to your blog is that it enables you to provide your subscribers with additional information without spending the time it takes to write it yourself. This is a huge enough benefit in itself. But I'll let you in on a couple of little secrets as to why I allow my guest bloggers to post links to the ecommerce sites where their books are sold: one, I can attach affiliate links to those books that allow me to earn a commission on those sales; and two, it increases the chances of people clicking on both *my* book(s) and *their* book(s) on an ecommerce site. Because it increases the chances of our books appearing on each other's ecommerce webpages under the "customers who viewed this item also viewed" and/or "frequently bought together" sections. This is one sneaky way you can make an algorithm work in your favour to increase both your sales.

What is Content Syndication?

Earlier in this chapter, we covered why regular blogging is such an important part of any author's online marketing plan. This is because it can improve the search engine optimization (SEO)—that is, the ranking and visibility—of your blog, or even the ecommerce site where your book is being sold, on top search engines such as Google and Baidu. It all depends on which webpage(s) you're promoting and redirecting traffic to within the content you're posting. When you improve the SEO for any webpage, you increase the chances of its target audience finding it.

An SEO Analogy: Retail Merchandising

When you think about it, SEO is a lot like effective merchandising in a "bricks and mortar" bookstore. It's all about positioning. The books that are strategically placed at eye level in the front aisles, or on shelving units and tables in the high-traffic areas of a store, are going to sell more than the books that are tucked away on low shelves where most people don't bother to look.

It works much the same way online. The whole point of improving the SEO of any webpage is to ensure it appears as close to the top of an online search as possible so that more people can easily see it. The higher its visibility, the better its chance of it being clicked on which translates into the better chance of a sale down the road. And that's what we're all after here, isn't it? At the end of the day, authors are blogging to promote their books with the intent of selling more copies and improving their readerships.

Here's the good news: it's somewhat easier—and much more cost effective—to improve your positioning online than it is within a traditional bookstore, particularly the major chain stores. If you want prime real estate in a major chain, allowing you to be seen by hundreds or even thousands of impulse buyers on any given day, you're going to have to pay upfront for the privilege. How much will it cost you? John B. Thompson provides details about this in his 2012 Kindle ebook titled *Merchants of Culture: The Publishing Business in the Twenty-First Century*:

> The front-of-store area that is in your field of vision is a thoroughly commodified space: most of the books you see will be there by virtue of the fact that the publisher has paid for placement, either directly by means of a placement fee (that is, co-op advertising) or indirectly by means of extra discount. Roughly speaking, it costs around a dollar a book to put a new hardback on the front-of-store table in a major chain, and around $10,000 to put a new title on front-of-store tables in all the chain's stores for two weeks (typically the minimum period). ... Visibility does not come cheap. (Thompson, 2012)

While you can choose to pay for increased exposure online by running PPC advertising campaigns or buying banner ads on high-traffic websites, the difference here is that you don't have to. Blogging is an organic—not to mention free—way of improving your online ranking. Your only cost is your time.

Don't Get Dinged by The SEO Gods!

Now, here's the kicker: all your online articles and blog posts must be original content. Why? Because also built into these search engine algorithms is the ability to detect copied/reused content—and copied/reused content is a no-no in the online world. It is treated almost like a form of plagiarism and "penalized" by search engines in the sense that it won't be indexed by them at all; rather, it will be ignored altogether. The search engines will compare two webpages that contain the same content and choose only one—most likely the original, higher ranking page—to include in search results. The copycat webpage will fall into online oblivion, never to be seen or heard from on the search engines again.

Content Syndication to The Rescue

The obvious issue here is *time*. Where is the time to write all your books, and write original articles for other online publications, and post unique content to your own blog on a regular basis so you can organically grow (and maintain) a strong online presence? Even the simple idea of it is daunting enough itself, never mind actually doing it day in and day out. We all have busy lives, after all.

This is where content syndication comes into play as explained by Christopher Ratcliff in his article titled "What is content syndication and how do I get started?" on the Search Engine Watch website. According to Ratcliff, content syndication is great for new authors and publishers who want to expose their books and blogs to a much larger audience, but who just don't have the time or manpower to write copious amounts of new content daily.

> Content syndication is the process of pushing your blogpost, article, video or any piece of web-based content out to other third-parties who will then republish it on their own sites….

> Content syndication is particularly useful if you're a smaller publisher or an up-and-coming writer who wants a larger audience from a more authoritative site.

> By having your blog content published on The Guardian (for instance) you will be exposed to a much

wider audience that isn't your own, who may then visit you on your own blog.

The other major reason for doing this is SEO. Some of that bigger site's authority should be passed down to you. (Ratcliff, 2016)

According to Ratcliff's article, search engines are intuitive when it comes to recognizing that text links refer back to the original post; so, that is usually enough to prevent the indexing issues that stem from duplicate content. But, whenever possible, HTML coding is generally the best solution—particularly rel=canonical tags—as we talked about earlier.

Finding the Right Content Syndication Partners for You

There are many potential syndication partners available to you depending on the field you're in and the content you're writing about. It will take a bit of time and research in the beginning. What you'll be looking for are publications that: one, write for a similar audience as you write for; and two, are interested in publishing syndicated content.

Free Syndication Options (Sprint)

One of the fastest, easiest ways to syndicate your blog content is to re-publish it yourself to any free high-traffic websites that you have immediate access to—which is why I refer to these options as "sprint" options. Even better if they are channels with significant distribution networks. Three such publication channels are LinkedIn, Quora, and Amazon Author Central pages.

- **Linkedin: Best for Business-Related Books and Blogs**
  As of January 2019, eBizMBA Guide (http://www.ebizmba.com/articles/social-networking-websites) rated LinkedIn as the 5th most popular social media site—after Facebook, YouTube, Twitter, and Instagram—with an estimated 250,000,000 unique visitors per month. That's a huge audience for business professionals of any kind, all over the world, and offers an outstanding opportunity to promote books and blogs. The Publications and LinkedIn Pulse Articles sections of this site are perfect tools for our purposes here.

  Your LinkedIn profile functions as an online resume. It is here, in the Publications section of your profile, that you can feature your published book(s). Better yet, you can move sections around. By moving Publications towards the top of your profile, and marking it as a public section, it will make your book(s) appear more prominent to everyone who looks at your profile page—even those who aren't your first connections.

  At the top of your profile page, you'll also notice another LinkedIn element known as Articles. This is the perfect place for you to either write unique content or share past blog posts and articles as syndicated content, as I've done here: https://www.linkedin.com/pulse/how-sell-books-linkedin-kim-staflund. You'll notice, at the top of the article, there is a place for readers to click on your profile page where they'll see your books displayed. From there, they can either send you a connection request or simply follow you on LinkedIn so that they receive notification of all your upcoming posts.

- **Quora: Great Networking Opportunities Here**

  Quora is, first and foremost, a question and answer site. It's free of charge to set up a profile on which you can promote a direct link to your blog and list any other important credentials or highlights that you wish to share. From there, you can either post questions for various other industry experts to answer for you; or, you can search for questions related to your industry that have been posted by others and provide them with well-thought-out, helpful answers. It's a great way to network with people all over the world and build up your brand's trust organically.

  But here we are again—doing more work to build our brands *organically*. It's more writing again, isn't it? Time consuming, right?

  Luckily, Quora has another feature you can utilize to post your syndicated content—which is great news because, according to a May 2017 post by the Search Engine Journal (https://www.searchenginejournal.com/what-is-quora-and-why-should-you-care/28475/), this Q&A site receives approximately 100,000,000 unique visitors per month. And it's growing in popularity all the time. What is this other feature I'm referring to? Quora allows you to create a blog on its site free of charge. Much like LinkedIn's Articles section, this is a great place for you to either write unique content or share past blog posts and articles as syndicated content as I've done here: https://kimstaflund.quora.com/Guest-Blogging-and-Content-Syndication-T-Shaped-Marketing-for-Authors. On the plus side, this site isn't limited to business-related content. Authors of poetry and fictional novels can benefit from this platform just as much as non-fiction writers can.

- **Amazon: Share Your Wordpress RSS Feed on Your Author Page**

  There's another great form of content syndication known as Really Simple Syndication (RSS) (http://rss.softwaregarden.com/aboutrss.html). If your main blog has an RSS feed like most (if not all) WordPress blogs do, then you can easily share teasers of your latest blog posts to your Amazon Author Central page as I've done here: https://www.amazon.com/Kim-Staflund/e/B0733M2PZV/. Not only is this a fantastic way to drive additional traffic to your blog via Amazon; but each time you make a change to your author page (e.g., by publishing a new book, adding a new photo, editing your author profile, posting a new blog teaser, et cetera), it acts as an update on Amazon. Frequent, relevant updates to a website are great ways to trigger Google's algorithm so your author page ranks higher in its search results over time.

As of this book's writing time, there are only five regions in the world that offer Author Central pages and you must set up each one separately from the rest: the USA, UK, Germany, France, and Japan. I've also found that only the USA page allows for links to RSS feeds, but I'm hopeful the other regions will begin to see the benefit of this and add it to their platforms over time.

LinkedIn, Quora, and Amazon are only three of the many free syndication options you can choose from. Who you work with—where you post your content to—largely depends on the audience you wish to reach. It also depends on whether you want to manually post an entire article or blog entry as shown in the LinkedIn Pulse and Quora samples, or if you prefer to have an RSS feed automatically submitted each time you post something new to your primary WordPress blog as shown in the Amazon Author Central sample.

Here is a list of some additional free content syndication tools: Tumblr, Disqus, ZergNet, Scoop.it, Hacker News, and Reddit. Reddit is one of the more popular ones that you've probably already heard of as this site covers many different topics from world news to gaming to television and the arts. There will most likely be a section on Reddit that fits well with your content—possibly even more than one.

Free Syndication Options (Marathon)

Another way to syndicate your content is to contact other bloggers and online publications who cover similar topic matter as you do. Rather than viewing them as competitors, look at them more as potential partners you can share and expand your respective audiences with. Keep in mind that content syndication of this kind is all about relationship building—and it's more of a marathon than a sprint to earn the trust of other people. You earn that trust by proving the value of your own work, acknowledging their work, and then recommending a mutually beneficial syndication partnership with them. But don't be alarmed if it takes a few tries before they go for it. Be persistent in a patient and respectful way, and you'll eventually break through.

Kevan Lee wrote a helpful post titled "How to Become a Columnist: The Ultimate Blueprint for Guest Blogging and Syndication" on the Buffer Social blog a while back that discussed how guest blogging can help lead to syndication opportunities with high-ranking online publications such as Huffington Post:

> The first step toward our syndication was guest blogging. And lots of it! Leo wrote around 150 guest posts in a nine-month period. The process was huge for spreading awareness about Buffer, building a relationship with influencers and a portfolio of quality writing, and establishing the Buffer blog as an authority on lifehacking and social media….
>
> When we chose to pitch a few sites on republishing our content, having huge hits like these gave us instant credibility. We shared our best stuff. In turn, the sites we pitched to received built-in validation that our posts would resonate with readers. (Lee, 2016)

Kevan goes on to talk about the various benefits to having your work shared by other publications. Doing so not only gives you more credibility as an authority on your topic matter, but it also opens you up to a whole new world of readers who may only stick to one publication. They would be missing out on your content if it wasn't shared with them by that publication.

For more information on how to approach content syndication opportunities of any kind, I highly recommend you read yet another article titled "Content Syndication: The Definitive, Insider's Guide" by Ritika Puri that was posted on The Buzzstream Blog a while back. One of the most helpful aspects of this post is her recommendation on how to word your pitch email to a potential new syndication partner as shown here:

Hey {Person},

I wanted to pass along a post that you might consider syndicating on your blog. It's one of our most popular posts, having generated X visits in the last Y days. Given our shared audience of social media managers, I think it could bring you a lot of additional traffic too.

Feel free to use it: just make sure to attribute the original source so we don't get dinged on the SEO front. (Puri, 2015)

That's a fantastic piece of advice that is missing from so many other sources on content syndication—how to actually *write* the pitch letter! Thanks Ritika! The only thing I'll add is exactly who the person is that she's referring to in her pitch letter—it's best to start with either the features editor or the contributions editor.

How Book Publicists Can Help You Score Guest Blogging and Content Syndication Opportunities with High-Ranking Publications

On my blog, I often discuss ways authors can market and sell your books using various forms of both free and paid online advertising. Now I'm going to talk about publicity. In her ebook titled *The Power of Publicity for Your Book*, Marsha Friedman provides us with a clear distinction between the two:

By definition, publicity is not advertising; it's coverage by the media of people, events and issues deemed to be of interest to their audiences.

...The nice thing about publicity, also referred to as "earned media," is that you don't buy it; you earn it. If you can get a journalist or talk show host interested in your story idea or topic, you might be interviewed for an article, asked to write an article for publication, or invited to be interviewed as a guest on a radio or TV show.

The endorsement of traditional media, even if it's simply mentioning your name, has always been marketing gold to anyone trying to build a reputation as an author and gain visibility for their book. (Friedman, n.d.)

Some authors misunderstand the role of publicists. They hire a publicity firm assuming that organization will advertise and sell their book(s) for them, but this is incorrect. The true role of a publicist is to garner publicity for their *client*—to get that author mentioned in the media via Associated Press-style articles and press releases written about the topic(s) in his or her book, and by promoting that author as an industry expert in his or her field. The idea is to attract newspaper, radio, and television interviews that will highlight the publicist's client within the mainstream media. The by-product of this publicity is a heightened interest in the author, which should boost sales of his or her book over time much like advertising does.

Both advertising and publicity are about putting yourself in front of a larger audience as often as possible to build on (and maintain) top-of-mind awareness with your current and prospective readers; but, by contrast, advertising is essentially you talking about yourself and your book whereas publicity is the *media* talking about you and your book. Obviously, when someone else is talking about you, it has more credibility in the eyes of the public. That's the power of publicity.

There is an additional benefit to hiring a publicist to help you find guest blogging and content syndication opportunities. Publicity firms have developed long-standing relationships with all the "movers and shakers" in the media, and their staff knows exactly how to format articles to have an "Associated Press" appeal that is more likely to be picked up. They watch the news regularly, so they're aware of what is going on and how to tie you and your book topics into current events. Hiring a publicist is somewhat expensive but, in my opinion, it's worth the investment when you're working with a reputable firm.

How expensive is it? Well, it depends. There are different types of publicists out there. Some firms want a retainer, much like a law firm, and they will charge their clients for time spent researching, writing, and contacting the media as well as for telephone charges, postage fees, and any other materials they create for you (i.e., printing and copying). And then there are the firms that use a pay-for-performance business model where they charge only one lump sum fee in the beginning and guarantee a certain amount of publicity along with that lump sum fee.

Six Important Questions to Ask a Book Publicist

When researching which book publicity firm to use, I recommend asking them all the following six questions for clarification.

1. Will you read my book? That sounds like an odd question to ask an organization you're hiring to help you promote yourself and your book, doesn't it? But it's an important question to ask. In my experience, many publicity firms *won't* read your book unless you

insist on it. Perhaps, they don't need to. Ask them for clarification about this.

2. What are your prices? Ask for a price list of all their program options, and ask what services are included in each program.

3. What additional costs are involved in this process: do you want additional postage fees sent to you upfront and/or throughout the campaign for sending out review copies; how many physical review copies do you want mailed to you ahead of time; do you send these review copies out to low-ranking individual bloggers or to high-ranking relevant media outlets?

4. How many of the interviewers you book for me will actually go through with the interview? Do any of them cancel at the last minute, after receiving the free review copy, and then post that book on Amazon for sale? (Believe it or not, this happens. And, yes, you're right—it's unacceptable.)

5. Do you expect to include my personal phone number and email address on the press release you send out to the media? Will you share that press release publicly online via your website and/or any other websites? How do you protect each author's privacy in this regard?

6. Will your firm find relevant and recognized media outlets who are willing to accept any guest posts I've written that link back to my own blog?

Start with those six questions and see where they take you. You'll learn a lot about the firm you're dealing with through them. Make your decision from there.

THE AUTHOR'S MONEY TREE SEASON #3: HARVESTING

Once you have planted enough seeds and grown a bountiful crop, you will have something special to harvest and share with a growing number of readers each year. It is only once you've done this that email marketing will be *truly* beneficial for you.

Engage with Your Readers in a More Personal Way

Today, most people are accessing their email messages on their smartphones just as often—if not oftener—than they do on their laptops or desktops. This is why email marketing is such an important component of mobile marketing, of *any* kind of marketing, for authors.

I was first introduced to email marketing in late 2016 when I came across a Facebook advertisement inviting me to download a free ebook titled *The Circle of Profit: How to Turn Your Passion into an Information Business* by Anik Singal. At that time, I'd been running my own digital book publishing company for seven years; and my dream, from the start, was to successfully operate this business in a virtual office environment so I could freely travel and work with anyone, anywhere in the world, at any given time. But building this online company proved to be quite a challenge. I was still having to work elsewhere, to support myself and pay my bills, because I wasn't generating enough business to earn a decent profit. I think that's why Anik's book caught my attention—because here was this pioneer of online marketing reaching out to me through the Internet, and he was willing to share his tried and true methods regarding how to turn my passion into a successful online business once and for all.

I devoured Anik's book in full over one weekend. I even read it a second time, the following week, to ensure I fully grasped every concept and recommendation he had to offer. It restored my passion and renewed my hope—along with providing actual statistics and a roadmap on how to do things right. It showed me I was already on the right track in many ways, and that I should stay the course.

> In 2012, Amazon CEO Jeff Bezos announced that Amazon's sales of digital books had surpassed their sales of physical books. Just look at how fast the Internet is growing around the world.

> In the last 10 years, the number of people using the Internet has grown by 600%. It's estimated that there are more than three billion people now with access to the Internet. (Singal, 2016)

According to Anik, there were only a few things I needed to tweak to get my online publishing business to take off once and for all; and, one of those things was to add email marketing into the mix. All these years, I'd been collecting email addresses through my blog and website. But I'd never utilized them in any way. I didn't know how. Anik was the first person to effectively explain the value of email marketing to me in a way that really resonated.

> Who do you trust more: a friend or a stranger? The answer is obvious: Your friend. And when your email list subscribers start seeing you more as a friend than some random person sending them emails, you'll get the best response. (Singal, 2016)

That's what email marketing is all about. It's a powerful vehicle that allows you to reach people in a more direct and personal way than other forms of online marketing can. It is your opportunity to really engage with your readers. Become their friend by letting them know a little more about you, the person, rather than just advertising your book(s) and business to them in an impersonal way. Spend some time getting to know them a little better by replying to their emailed questions with thoughtful answers.

And Anik Singal isn't the only person who swears by email marketing. While I was researching bestselling strategies for authors, I came across an online *Forbes* article by Jay McGregor titled "Amazon Pays $450,000 A Year To This Self-Published Writer." That's when I was first introduced to a UK author named Mark Dawson who was selling massive quantities of books online, and who was more than willing to openly share his success strategies during that interview. A flame lit inside my heart when I read Mark's take on email marketing because it matched perfectly with what I'd read in Anik's book earlier. It confirmed for me that I was *definitely* on the right track.

> Dawson also credits his success to his unusual attitude towards publishing. He approaches it like a business, one in which writing is just a single cog in the media machine. He engages (responding to all fan messages) with all of his fans and focusses on building a rapport to ensure their loyalty. He holds seminars to give other writers advice and guidance. And through all of these activities, he collects names and email addresses that have amounted to a 15,000 person strong mailing list. It's through this that he disseminates his new work. What Dawson has done is

essentially build a small but loyal community that translates into near guaranteed sales. (McGregor, 2015)

The readers who know and trust you will be your most responsive buyers each time you contact them to announce a new book, product, or service of any kind. Just ask Anik Singal and Mark Dawson. But this trust must be earned over time by providing quality, valuable content to your subscribers on a consistent basis so they stay engaged with you over the long term. That's why you must plant and grow a *bountiful* crop before you try to harvest it. Always remember there are no "quick and easy" fixes in the world of online marketing. Stay focused. Be patient with the process. Be patient with yourself. But *never* give up, because your efforts will be rewarded greatly if you stay the course.

How does email marketing work? Quite simply, you want to drive increasing amounts of traffic to your blog by consistently posting new content to it that makes people want to stay engaged. You also want these people to "opt-in" to receive email notices every time you post something new there.

Not only must you obtain an official "opt-in" from every person before you can send him or her a marketing email of any kind; you must also, by law, include an "opt-out" option (also known as an unsubscribe link) at the bottom of each email you send. This is governed by the Controlling the Assault of Non-Solicited Pornography and Marketing (CAN-SPAM) act in the United States and the Canadian Anti-Spam Law (CASL) in Canada to prevent the overuse or abuse of this marketing technology. All other countries should have similar laws in place. Ensure you're properly following the regulations in your area.

What is the Difference Between Blog Subscribers versus Registered Users?

WordPress is kind of sneaky in the way it interchanges the words "registered users" (also referred to as *team* members in WordPress lingo) and "subscribers" (also referred to as *followers* in WordPress lingo) on its administrative platforms. But it's important that you never mix up these terms as per the CAN-SPAM and CASL laws mentioned earlier. Carol Manser wrote a great article about this titled "Registered Users, Subscribers & Logins: What's the Difference?" Here's what she has to say about the difference between the two:

> If someone Registers on a website, they become Registered Users. Unless the site tells you that you will get some extra privilege for Registering, you will get no extra benefit from Registering.
>
> A common reason why you might want to Register on a website, is Registering on a Forum. You usually have to Register on a Forum before you are allowed to Post questions on the Forum.
>
> If someone Subscribes to a website, they consent to be put onto an Email List in exchange for whatever the website has offered to give them in exchange for their Name and Email Address details. Because of this Consent/Confirmation to receive Emails, Subscribing to a Website is not the same as Registering with a site. (Manser, 2013)

It is important to understand that when someone "registers" to your WordPress site, all they're agreeing to is the right to post comments to your blog as shown in this illustration:

META

Register ⬅ Here is where people register for the right to post comments to your blog.

Log in

Entries RSS

Comments RSS

WordPress.org

[ ] Search

Unfortunately, WordPress lists these registered users as "subscribers" on your blog's admin area dashboard as shown here:

🏠 PPG Publisher's Blog 💬 0 ➕ New 🅈

Users [Add New] [Export Users]

All (12,273) | Administrator (1) | Subscriber (12,272)

But this wording is inaccurate. Of these 12,272 people (plus me, I'm the Administrator) who are registered to be able to comment on my posts, only nine of them are actual subscribers/followers who have specifically signed up to receive updates each time I publish a new post:

Followers (9)

The other 12,263 registered users won't receive an email update when I post something new, so they're not all that useful to me at harvest time. They may never visit my blog again.

What you need are actual subscribers—*email* subscribers—who have signed up specifically to receive email updates from you. There are a couple of ways you can achieve this. First, you can replace the META widget (shown earlier) with the following SUBSCRIBER widget in your design template:

SUBSCRIBE TO THE PPG PUBLISHER'S BLOG VIA EMAIL

Enter your email address to subscribe to this blog and receive notifications of new posts by email.

Email Address

Subscribe

Anyone who signs up through that form is showing *real* interest in your blog content and books. Each time you post something new, he or she will be made aware of it with a personal email. This will dramatically improve your reader engagement.

But there is a second, possibly even better, way to collect a growing number of email subscribers who will repeatedly visit both your blog *and* your books. You will want to follow Anik Singal's lead by using a program called an autoresponder to manage all your email subscribers. MailChimp for WordPress is free for lists up to 2,000 subscribers. After that, depending on the service you use, autoresponders generally cost from $50 per month and up to maintain. It all depends on how many email addresses you are working with.

> The email addresses you collect on your opt-in page do not sit on your own computer. They actually fly into a database automatically, using a copy-and paste line of code that you've put on your page. This database of email addresses is called an autoresponder.

> There are many third party companies, which will manage the entire autoresponder process for you. It's incredibly easy. They give you a line of code that you simply copy and paste into your opt-in page. Instantly, the email addresses that your visitors enter are automatically placed into your autoresponder. (Singal, 2016)

Through these third parties, such as MailChimp, you can offer additional special discounts or gifts to subscribers on top of the free content already contained on your blog. For example, you can send private newsletters en masse to only these privileged fans regarding online courses or podcasts that constitute some type of added value to them alone. Perhaps, these subscribers will be the only ones to receive discounts on tickets (or back stage passes) to the next book fair you're speaking at. I think you get the idea. For this to work well, there must be an enticing reason for them to sign up—whatever that reason may be. You choose.

Add *This* to Blogging and Watch Your Book Sales Soar Even Higher

Very early on, I stated that there are three effective ways to plant an abundance of seeds with your desired readership: productive blogging, prolific publishing, or (better yet) *both*. Ed Pilkington illustrated the value of prolific publishing rather well in his article titled "Amanda Hocking, the writer who made millions by self-publishing online" that was published in *The Guardian* online a few years back.

> In 2009 she went into overdrive. She was frantic to get her first book published by the time she was 26, the age Stephen King was first in print, and time was running out (she's now 27). So while holding down a day job caring for severely disabled people, for which she earned $18,000 a year, she went into a Red Bull-fuelled frenzy of writing at night, starting at 8pm and continuing until dawn. Once she got going, she could write a complete novel in just two or three weeks. By the start of 2010, she had amassed a total of 17 unpublished novels, all gathering digital dust on the desktop of her laptop. (Pilkington, 2012)

The article goes on to describe how, in April of 2010, she published the first of many fictional novels to a few different online platforms and saw sales of roughly nine copies per day as a result. A few weeks later, she published two more novels and saw her monthly sales grow to *hundreds* of books. A few more weeks after that, she published a fourth novel online and was amazed to see her book sales increase into the *thousands* that month! Long story short, she continued publishing every few weeks, and her sales continued to multiply accordingly. The rest is history.

Granted, Amanda's is a rather extreme success story. But the techniques she used to inadvertently become a millionaire—the top two being prolific writing and publishing—are the same techniques many others continue to use with great success to this day, whether they are writing fiction or non-fiction. Sometimes, it simply takes a few more books and a bit more time, as was the case for this non-fiction success story, Steve Scott:

> Steve talks about splitting big topics into micro-topics, which stems from his blogging background. His books are around 15,000 – 25,000 words and delve deep, rather than being the 'be all and end all' megabook which is more like the traditional publishing model.

> ...The tipping point into a full time income came when Steve fully committed himself to the model of Kindle publishing in Sept 2012, and wrote a book every 3 weeks. The tipping point to the big league earnings was in May 2014 when Habit Stacking took off, and having 40+ books available helped make more income from the back list. Focus on the genre and the niche and write content within that and build up a brand and a series. Be consistent in your writing. Make it a habit. (Penn 01, 2014)

You see? Whether you write fiction like James Patterson or non-fiction like Steve Scott, you *can* see sales success with smaller books. Throw away any pre-conceived notions you may have about what constitutes a useful book—particularly when it comes to word count. I'm here to tell you that it's more important to focus on the *quality* of your content than the *quantity* of words you've written. There is absolutely no need to add a bunch of unnecessary fluff into a book just to get it to a certain word count. Basing a book's value and saleability on word count is old-fashioned thinking. Today, you want to write for the search engines; take that 90,000-word novel you wrote and break it into a three-ebook mini-series instead. Maybe even a six-ebook series! You'll get much more bang for your buck that way.

Throughout this book, I've highlighted various authors who are seeing *significant* success in terms of the volumes of books they're selling online every single year. These four, in particular, have earned six- or seven-figure annual incomes from their ebook sales and have openly shared their stories in prominent online publications:

- Amanda Hocking was one of the first reported Amazon millionaires who utilized prolific publishing (releasing a new book online at least every six weeks, if not oftener) to self-publish her fictional books after multiple rejections by the traditional trade publishers. Of her success, Ed Pilkington wrote in *The Guardian*:

    > When historians come to write about the digital transformation currently engulfing the book-publishing world, they will almost certainly refer to Amanda Hocking, writer of paranormal fiction who in the past 18 months has emerged from obscurity to bestselling status entirely under her own self-published steam. (Pilkington, 2012)

- Mark Dawson, by contrast, was first trade published. But when he saw how few copies his publisher sold of his fictional novel, he switched to self-publishing and learned how to become an *entrepreneurial* author instead. Of his six-figure success, Jay McGregor wrote in *Forbes*:

> Dawson's recent success isn't representative of his time in publishing, however. He actually had a book published by Pan Books called 'The Art of Falling Apart' in 2000, which completely bombed. Not because it was bad - ironically it's now available on Kindle and has 32 five-star reviews out of 39 - but because few people read it or are aware of it. Mark puts the book's failure down to the publishers inability to promote his work and generate any sort of interest." (McGregor, 2015)

- Steve Scott is a notable non-fiction success story, proving this "rapid release" technique can work for all kinds of books—not only fictional novels. Of his success, Joanna Penn wrote on The Creative Penn blog:

> If you want a six figure income from your books, it's a good idea to model people who are already making this kind of money. Steve Scott seemed to burst onto the indie non-fiction scene in early 2014, but in fact, he has 42 books and has had an internet business since 2006. (Penn 01, 2014)

- And then there is Joanna Penn herself. I'm certain you'll fall in love with her story, as I have, if you spend enough time reading her blog posts and watching her podcast on The Creative Penn blog. Not only is Joanna personable, but she's also so willing to share her honest journey with budding authors—to show you not only what it takes, but that it *is* possible to get to where she is:

> All authors start with a blank page and no audience. You don't get from first word to multi-six-figures overnight, but it can be done if you are persistent and productive over time. Here are the significant steps on my journey from writing my first book while working at my corporate day job to multi-six-figure author entrepreneur. (Penn 02, n.d.)

These four success stories confirm what I've been writing about and teaching to aspiring and established authors alike for several years now: the most successful authors are the ones who treat book writing, publishing, sales, and marketing as their own businesses. They don't only write; they *sell* their own books. So, although I'm sharing examples of independent authors with you here, please know this book can be equally helpful to traditionally-published authors. You can take the same steps to turbo-charge your publisher's marketing efforts; you can prevent a frontlist title from moving to the backlist by keeping it in front of your readers longer, just like these independent authors all do. The proof is in these pages. Good luck!

BIBLIOGRAPHY

Alter, A. (2016, March 21). *James Patterson Has a Big Plan for Small Books*. Retrieved from The New York Times: https://www.nytimes.com/2016/03/22/business/media/james-patterson-has-a-big-plan-for-small-books.html

Altman, I. (2015, December 1). *Top 10 Business Trends That Will Drive Success In 2016*. Retrieved from Forbes: https://www.forbes.com/sites/ianaltman/2015/12/01/top-10-business-trends-that-will-drive-success-in-2016/#5b06ccc358ea

Clarke, A. (2018). In *SEO 2018: Learn Search Engine Optimization With Smart Internet Marketing Strategies. [Kindle version]*. United States: Simple Effectiveness Publishing. Available from Amazon.com.

Friedman, M. (n.d.). *The Power of Publicity for Your Book*. Retrieved from News and Experts (formerly EMSI Public Relations): http://newsandexperts.com/wp-content/uploads/2014/03/Power-of-Publicity-for-Your-Book.pdf

LaRocca, M. (2019, January 16). *Finding the Best Way to Write*. Retrieved from PPG Publisher's Blog: https://blog.polishedpublishinggroup.com/2019/01/finding-the-best-way-to-write/

Lee, K. (2016, March 21). *How to Become a Columnist: The Ultimate Blueprint for Guest Blogging and Syndication*. Retrieved from Buffer Social: https://blog.bufferapp.com/how-to-become-a-columnist-guest-posting-syndication

Manser, C. (2013). *Registered Users, Subscribers & Logins: What's the Difference?* Retrieved from My Second Million! How to Set Up a Blog and Make Money Online: http://www.mysecondmillion.com/register-subscribe-login/

McGregor, J. (2015, April 17). *Amazon Pays $450,000 A Year To This Self-Published Writer*. Retrieved from Forbes: https://www.forbes.com/sites/jaymcgregor/2015/04/17/mark-dawson-made-750000-from-self-published-amazon-books/#5985abab6b5b

MOZ. (n.d.). *What is SEO?* Retrieved from SEO Learning Center: https://moz.com/learn/seo/what-is-seo

Penn 01, J. (2014, October 14). *Six Figure Success Self-Publishing Non-Fiction Books With Steve Scott*. Retrieved from The Creative Penn: https://www.thecreativepenn.com/2014/10/14/non-fiction-success/

Penn 02, J. (n.d.). *My Author Timeline. From First Book To Multi-Six-Figure Author Entrepreneur*. Retrieved from The Creative Penn: https://www.thecreativepenn.com/timeline/

Pilkington, E. (2012, January 12). *Amanda Hocking, the writer who made millions by self-publishing online*. Retrieved from The Guardian: https://www.theguardian.com/books/2012/jan/12/amanda-hocking-self-publishing

Puri, R. (2015, September 16). *Content Syndication: The Definitive, Insider's Guide*. Retrieved from BuzzStream Blog: https://www.buzzstream.com/blog/content-syndication-the-definitive-insiders-guide.html

Ratcliff, C. (2016, August 3). *Search Engine Watch*. Retrieved from What is content syndication and how do I get started?: https://searchenginewatch.com/2016/08/03/what-is-content-syndication-and-how-do-i-get-started/

Singal, A. (2016). *The Circle of Profit: How to Turn Your Passion into an Information Business*. Retrieved from Lurn, Inc. (www.lurn.com): http://circleofprofit.s3.amazonaws.com/The_Circle_of_Profit.pdf

Thompson, J. B. (2012). *Merchants of Culture: The Publishing Business in the Twenty-First Century Second Edition*. Cambridge, UK: Polity Press. Kindle Edition.

Yoast. (2018, December 24). *rel=canonical: the ultimate guide*. Retrieved from Yoast SEO for everyone: https://yoast.com/rel-canonical/

INDEX

ABOUT THE AUTHOR

So many people are publishing books of all kinds nowadays, and they need guidance regarding best practices with everything from writing to publishing to selling those books. I've made it my life's mission to help others navigate this mysterious business littered with acronyms and peculiar old-fashioned practices.

As a bestselling author and TESOL-certified sales coach for authors with 25 years' experience in the North American English book publishing industry (in both the traditional and contemporary markets), I can show you how to write, publish, and sell your book(s) using all the effective traditional and online tricks of the trade. Add my substantial advertising sales and marketing background into the mix, and you have a serious mentor in front of you who can help you achieve commercial success as an author.

If your goal is to produce a professional quality book that you can sell commercially, the team at Polished Publishing Group (PPG) can help. We teach authors how to write a book, how to publish a book, how to sell a book. Professional project management services are also available.

Visit my company website here:
https://polishedpublishinggroup.com/

Visit my blog here:
https://blog.polishedpublishinggroup.com/